EMMANUEL JOSEPH

Unseen Stakeholders, the Role of Microorganisms in Sustainable Business Practices

Copyright © 2025 by Emmanuel Joseph

All rights reserved. No part of this publication may be reproduced, stored or transmitted in any form or by any means, electronic, mechanical, photocopying, recording, scanning, or otherwise without written permission from the publisher. It is illegal to copy this book, post it to a website, or distribute it by any other means without permission.

First edition

This book was professionally typeset on Reedsy.
Find out more at reedsy.com

Contents

1. Chapter 1: The Invisible Architects — 1
2. Chapter 2: The Microbial Economy — 3
3. Chapter 3: Waste Not, Want Not — 5
4. Chapter 4: The Green Factories — 7
5. Chapter 5: The Ethics of Microbial Exploitation — 9
6. Chapter 6: The Future of Food — 11
7. Chapter 7: The Power of Symbiosis — 13
8. Chapter 8: The Microbial Blueprint — 15
9. Chapter 9: The Invisible Guardians — 17
10. Chapter 10: The Microbial Revolution — 19
11. Chapter 11: The Business of Biodiversity — 21
12. Chapter 12: A New Partnership — 23

1

Chapter 1: The Invisible Architects

Microorganisms are the unseen architects of life on Earth, silently shaping ecosystems and enabling the survival of countless species, including humans. These tiny life forms—bacteria, fungi, algae, and more—have existed for billions of years, long before humans walked the planet. They are the foundation of life, driving processes like decomposition, nutrient cycling, and oxygen production. Yet, their role in business and sustainability has only recently begun to be appreciated. This chapter introduces the concept of microorganisms as silent stakeholders, exploring how they influence industries and why their potential is only now being unlocked.

In the natural world, microorganisms are the ultimate recyclers. They break down organic matter, turning waste into nutrients that sustain plants and animals. This process is not just vital for ecosystems but also holds immense value for businesses. Companies are beginning to see how microbial processes can transform waste management, reduce pollution, and create circular economies. By mimicking nature's systems, businesses can align their operations with the principles of sustainability, ensuring that resources are used efficiently and waste is minimized.

The relationship between humans and microorganisms is ancient. From fermenting food to producing antibiotics, we have long relied on these tiny allies. However, the industrial revolution shifted the focus to mechanical and chemical solutions, often at the expense of the environment. Today, as the world grapples with climate change and resource depletion, there is a renewed interest in microbial solutions. This chapter sets the stage for understanding how microorganisms can help businesses transition to more sustainable practices.

Microorganisms are not just tools; they are partners in sustainability. They thrive in diverse environments, from the depths of the ocean to the soil beneath our feet. Their adaptability and resilience make them ideal candidates for addressing complex challenges like pollution, energy production, and food security. By harnessing their capabilities, businesses can create innovative solutions that benefit both the economy and the planet. This chapter invites readers to rethink their perception of microorganisms, not as mere biological entities but as key players in the future of sustainable business.

The journey of understanding microorganisms as silent stakeholders begins with recognizing their ubiquity and importance. They are everywhere, yet often overlooked. As we delve deeper into their role in business, it becomes clear that these tiny organisms hold the key to solving some of the most pressing challenges of our time. This chapter lays the foundation for exploring how microorganisms can transform industries and pave the way for a more sustainable future.

2

Chapter 2: The Microbial Economy

The microbial economy is an emerging concept that highlights the economic value of microorganisms in various industries. From agriculture to biotechnology, these tiny organisms drive processes that are worth billions of dollars annually. In agriculture, microbes enhance soil fertility, reduce the need for chemical fertilizers, and improve crop yields. In the pharmaceutical industry, they are used to produce life-saving drugs, vaccines, and enzymes. This chapter explores the economic impact of microorganisms and how businesses can leverage their capabilities to create sustainable value.

One of the most significant contributions of microorganisms to the economy is in waste management. Traditional methods of waste disposal are often costly and environmentally harmful. Microbes offer a natural alternative, breaking down organic waste into useful byproducts like biogas and compost. Companies are increasingly adopting microbial technologies to manage waste more efficiently, reducing their environmental footprint while generating economic benefits. This chapter examines how businesses are integrating microbial solutions into their operations, creating a win-win scenario for both the economy and the environment.

The potential of the microbial economy extends beyond waste management. In the energy sector, microorganisms are being used to produce biofuels, offering a renewable alternative to fossil fuels. In the manufacturing sector, they are used to create bioplastics, reducing reliance on petroleum-based plastics. These innovations not only address environmental challenges but also open up new markets and revenue streams for businesses. This chapter highlights the diverse applications of microorganisms in the economy, showcasing their potential to drive sustainable growth.

However, the microbial economy is not without its challenges. Scaling up microbial technologies requires significant investment in research and infrastructure. There are also regulatory and ethical considerations to address, particularly when it comes to genetically modified organisms. This chapter discusses the barriers to realizing the full potential of the microbial economy and explores strategies for overcoming them. Collaboration between businesses, governments, and research institutions is essential to unlock the economic and environmental benefits of microorganisms.

The microbial economy represents a paradigm shift in how we think about sustainability. By viewing microorganisms as valuable resources, businesses can create innovative solutions that address both economic and environmental challenges. This chapter underscores the importance of investing in microbial technologies and fostering a culture of innovation. As we move forward, the microbial economy will play an increasingly important role in shaping a sustainable future.

3

Chapter 3: Waste Not, Want Not

Waste is one of the most pressing challenges facing businesses today. Traditional methods of waste disposal, such as landfills and incineration, are not only costly but also harmful to the environment. Microorganisms offer a natural solution to this problem, breaking down waste into useful byproducts like biogas, compost, and clean water. This chapter explores how businesses are using microbial technologies to transform waste management and create circular economies.

One of the most promising applications of microorganisms in waste management is anaerobic digestion. This process uses microbes to break down organic waste in the absence of oxygen, producing biogas that can be used as a renewable energy source. Companies in the food and agriculture industries are increasingly adopting anaerobic digestion to manage their waste more sustainably. This chapter examines case studies of businesses that have successfully implemented this technology, highlighting the economic and environmental benefits.

Another area where microorganisms are making a difference is in bioremediation. This process uses microbes to clean up contaminated sites, such as oil spills and industrial waste dumps. By breaking down pollutants into harmless substances, microorganisms can restore ecosystems and reduce the environmental impact of industrial activities. This chapter explores how businesses are using bioremediation to address pollution and meet regulatory requirements, showcasing the potential of microbial solutions to create a cleaner, healthier planet.

Composting is another example of how microorganisms can turn waste into a valuable resource. By breaking down organic matter into nutrient-rich compost, microbes help improve soil health and reduce the need for chemical fertilizers. Businesses in the agriculture and landscaping industries are increasingly using composting to manage organic waste and enhance sustainability. This chapter discusses the benefits of composting and how businesses can integrate it into their operations.

The use of microorganisms in waste management is not just about reducing waste; it's about creating value from what was once considered useless. By harnessing the power of microbes, businesses can transform waste into resources, reducing their environmental footprint and creating new revenue streams. This chapter concludes by emphasizing the importance of microbial technologies in building a circular economy, where waste is minimized, and resources are used efficiently.

4

Chapter 4: The Green Factories

The concept of green factories revolves around using biological processes to manufacture products in an environmentally friendly manner. Microorganisms are at the heart of this revolution, enabling the production of biofuels, bioplastics, and bio-based chemicals. This chapter explores how businesses are using microbial technologies to create green factories, reducing their reliance on fossil fuels and minimizing their environmental impact.

One of the most exciting applications of microorganisms in green factories is the production of biofuels. Microbes can convert organic matter into ethanol, biodiesel, and other renewable fuels, offering a sustainable alternative to fossil fuels. Companies in the energy sector are investing heavily in microbial biofuel production, recognizing its potential to reduce greenhouse gas emissions and combat climate change. This chapter examines the challenges and opportunities associated with microbial biofuels, highlighting the need for continued innovation and investment.

Bioplastics are another area where microorganisms are making a difference. Unlike traditional plastics, which are derived from petroleum, bioplastics are made from renewable resources like corn starch and sugarcane. Microbes play a key role in the production process, breaking down these raw materials into polymers that can be used to make biodegradable plastics. This chapter explores how businesses are using microbial technologies to produce bioplastics, reducing their reliance on petroleum-based plastics and addressing the global plastic waste crisis.

In addition to biofuels and bioplastics, microorganisms are also being used to produce bio-based chemicals. These chemicals, which are derived from renewable resources, offer a sustainable alternative to petrochemicals. Companies in the chemical industry are increasingly turning to microbial fermentation to produce bio-based chemicals, reducing their environmental impact and creating new market opportunities. This chapter discusses the potential of bio-based chemicals to transform the chemical industry and drive sustainable growth.

The transition to green factories is not without its challenges. Scaling up microbial technologies requires significant investment in research and infrastructure. There are also regulatory and ethical considerations to address, particularly when it comes to genetically modified organisms. This chapter explores the barriers to realizing the full potential of green factories and discusses strategies for overcoming them. Collaboration between businesses, governments, and research institutions is essential to unlock the economic and environmental benefits of microbial technologies.

Green factories represent the future of sustainable manufacturing. By harnessing the power of microorganisms, businesses can create innovative solutions that address both economic and environmental challenges. This chapter concludes by emphasizing the importance of investing in microbial technologies and fostering a culture of innovation. As we move forward, green factories will play an increasingly important role in shaping a sustainable future.

5

Chapter 5: The Ethics of Microbial Exploitation

As businesses increasingly turn to microorganisms for sustainable solutions, ethical questions arise. Is it right to exploit these tiny life forms for human gain? What are the potential consequences of manipulating microbial ecosystems? This chapter delves into the ethical considerations surrounding the use of microorganisms in business, exploring the balance between harnessing their capabilities and respecting their role in the natural world.

One of the key ethical concerns is the potential impact of microbial technologies on ecosystems. While microorganisms offer innovative solutions to environmental challenges, their widespread use could have unintended consequences. For example, the release of genetically modified microbes into the environment could disrupt natural ecosystems and harm biodiversity. This chapter examines the risks associated with microbial technologies and discusses the need for responsible research and development.

Another ethical consideration is the ownership and control of microbial resources. Microorganisms are a shared resource, found in every corner of the planet. However, the commercialization of microbial technologies raises questions about who should benefit from their use. Should profits from microbial innovations be shared with the communities where these organisms are found? This chapter explores the ethical implications of microbial exploitation and discusses the need for fair and equitable practices.

The use of microorganisms in business also raises questions about consent and agency. Unlike humans or animals, microorganisms cannot give consent or express their needs. This raises ethical questions about the extent to which we should manipulate these organisms for our benefit. This chapter delves into the philosophical and ethical debates surrounding the use of microorganisms, highlighting the need for a thoughtful and respectful approach.

Finally, this chapter emphasizes the importance of transparency and accountability in the use of microbial technologies. Businesses must be open about their practices and the potential risks associated with microbial innovations. They must also be accountable for any harm caused by their actions, whether to ecosystems or communities. This chapter concludes by calling for a holistic approach to ethics, one that considers the interests of all stakeholders, including microorganisms.

The ethical use of microorganisms is not just a moral imperative; it is also essential for the long-term success of sustainable business practices. By respecting the role of microorganisms in the natural world and addressing the ethical challenges associated with their use, businesses can create innovative solutions that benefit both humanity and the planet. This chapter invites readers to reflect on the ethical dimensions of microbial exploitation and consider how we can harness the power of microorganisms in a responsible and sustainable way.

6

Chapter 6: The Future of Food

The global food system is under immense pressure to meet the demands of a growing population while minimizing its environmental impact. Microorganisms offer a promising solution to this challenge, revolutionizing the way we produce and consume food. From lab-grown meat to microbial protein, these tiny organisms are at the forefront of sustainable food innovation. This chapter explores how microorganisms are shaping the future of food and what it means for businesses and consumers alike.

One of the most exciting developments in the food industry is the use of microorganisms to produce alternative proteins. Companies are harnessing the power of microbes to create protein-rich foods that are sustainable, nutritious, and environmentally friendly. For example, microbial fermentation can produce protein powders that serve as a viable alternative to animal-based proteins. This chapter examines the potential of microbial protein to address food security and reduce the environmental impact of traditional agriculture.

Another area where microorganisms are making a difference is in the production of fermented foods. Fermentation, a process driven by microbes, has been used for centuries to preserve and enhance the nutritional value of food. Today, businesses are leveraging fermentation to create innovative products like plant-based cheeses, yogurts, and meat substitutes. This chapter explores how fermentation is being used to meet the growing demand for sustainable and healthy food options.

Microorganisms are also playing a key role in reducing food waste. By breaking down organic matter, microbes can transform food waste into valuable resources like compost and biogas. Companies in the food industry are increasingly adopting microbial technologies to manage waste more efficiently, reducing their environmental footprint and creating new revenue streams. This chapter highlights the potential of microorganisms to create a circular food economy, where waste is minimized, and resources are used efficiently.

However, the adoption of microbial technologies in the food industry is not without its challenges. Consumer acceptance, regulatory hurdles, and scalability are all barriers that must be addressed. This chapter discusses the challenges associated with microbial food innovations and explores strategies for overcoming them. Collaboration between businesses, researchers, and policymakers is essential to unlock the full potential of microorganisms in the food industry.

The future of food is being shaped by microorganisms, offering innovative solutions to some of the most pressing challenges of our time. By harnessing the power of microbes, businesses can create sustainable, nutritious, and delicious food products that benefit both people and the planet. This chapter concludes by emphasizing the importance of investing in microbial food technologies and fostering a culture of innovation in the food industry.

7

Chapter 7: The Power of Symbiosis

S ymbiosis, the close relationship between different biological species, is a fundamental principle of nature. In the business world, symbiosis can be seen in the collaboration between companies and microorganisms. This chapter explores the concept of industrial symbiosis, where waste from one process becomes the input for another, facilitated by microorganisms. It highlights examples of businesses that have embraced this approach, creating closed-loop systems that minimize waste and maximize efficiency.

One of the most compelling examples of industrial symbiosis is the use of microorganisms to create circular economies. In a circular economy, waste is not seen as a problem but as a resource. Microbes play a key role in this process, breaking down waste into useful byproducts like biogas, compost, and clean water. This chapter examines how businesses are using microbial technologies to create circular economies, reducing their environmental footprint and creating new revenue streams.

Another example of symbiosis in business is the use of microbial consortia, or communities of microorganisms, to achieve specific goals. For instance, in agriculture, microbial consortia can be used to enhance soil health, improve crop yields, and reduce the need for chemical fertilizers. This chapter explores how businesses are leveraging microbial consortia to create sustainable agricultural practices, benefiting both the economy and the environment.

The concept of symbiosis also extends to cross-industry collaboration. By working together, businesses from different sectors can create symbiotic networks that benefit all parties involved. For example, a brewery might partner with a biogas company to turn its waste into renewable energy. This chapter highlights the potential for cross-industry collaboration, showcasing how businesses can work together to create sustainable solutions.

However, achieving symbiosis in business is not without its challenges. It requires a shift in mindset, from viewing waste as a problem to seeing it as an opportunity. It also requires investment in research and infrastructure to develop and scale microbial technologies. This chapter discusses the barriers to achieving industrial symbiosis and explores strategies for overcoming them. Collaboration between businesses, governments, and research institutions is essential to unlock the full potential of microbial symbiosis.

The power of symbiosis lies in its ability to create win-win scenarios for businesses and the environment. By working with microorganisms, businesses can create innovative solutions that address both economic and environmental challenges. This chapter concludes by emphasizing the importance of embracing symbiosis as a guiding principle for sustainable business practices.

8

Chapter 8: The Microbial Blueprint

Nature has been perfecting sustainable practices for billions of years, and microorganisms are the architects of this success. This chapter explores how businesses can learn from microbial strategies to design more sustainable processes. From energy efficiency to resource optimization, microorganisms offer a blueprint for innovation. The chapter discusses biomimicry, the practice of emulating nature's designs and processes, and how it can be applied to business.

One of the key lessons businesses can learn from microorganisms is the importance of efficiency. Microbes are masters of resource optimization, using every available molecule to its fullest potential. For example, in anaerobic digestion, microbes break down organic matter into biogas with remarkable efficiency. This chapter examines how businesses can apply this principle to their operations, reducing waste and maximizing resource use.

Another lesson from microorganisms is the value of adaptability. Microbes thrive in diverse environments, from the depths of the ocean to the soil beneath our feet. Their ability to adapt to changing conditions is a testament to their resilience. This chapter explores how businesses can emulate this adaptability, creating flexible and resilient systems that can withstand environmental and economic challenges.

Microorganisms also demonstrate the power of collaboration. In nature, microbes often work together in communities to achieve common goals. For example, in the human gut, a diverse community of microbes works together to digest food and maintain health. This chapter discusses how businesses can foster a culture of collaboration, both within their organizations and with external partners, to achieve sustainable outcomes.

However, applying the microbial blueprint to business is not without its challenges. It requires a deep understanding of microbial processes and a commitment to innovation. This chapter explores the barriers to adopting biomimicry in business and discusses strategies for overcoming them. Collaboration between biologists, engineers, and business leaders is essential to unlock the full potential of microbial-inspired solutions.

The microbial blueprint offers a roadmap for sustainable business practices, rooted in the principles of efficiency, adaptability, and collaboration. By learning from microorganisms, businesses can create innovative solutions that address both economic and environmental challenges. This chapter concludes by emphasizing the importance of embracing biomimicry as a guiding principle for sustainable innovation.

9

Chapter 9: The Invisible Guardians

Microorganisms are not just tools for sustainability; they are also guardians of the environment. They play a crucial role in maintaining the health of ecosystems, from the soil to the oceans. This chapter explores the environmental services provided by microorganisms, such as carbon sequestration, nitrogen cycling, and water purification. It discusses how businesses can support these natural processes, rather than disrupt them, through sustainable practices.

One of the most important roles of microorganisms is in carbon sequestration. Microbes in the soil and oceans capture and store carbon, helping to mitigate climate change. This chapter examines how businesses can support microbial carbon sequestration, for example, by adopting regenerative agricultural practices that enhance soil health. It also explores the potential for microbial technologies to capture and store carbon in industrial settings.

Another critical role of microorganisms is in nitrogen cycling. Microbes convert nitrogen into forms that plants can use, supporting agricultural productivity. However, human activities like the overuse of chemical fertilizers can disrupt this process, leading to environmental problems like water pollution. This chapter discusses how businesses can support microbial nitrogen cycling, for example, by using organic fertilizers and adopting sustainable farming practices.

Microorganisms also play a key role in water purification. In natural ecosystems, microbes break down pollutants and purify water, maintaining the health of aquatic environments. This chapter explores how businesses can support microbial water purification, for example, by using constructed wetlands to treat wastewater. It also highlights the potential for microbial technologies to address water pollution in industrial settings.

However, supporting the role of microorganisms as environmental guardians requires a shift in mindset. Businesses must recognize the value of microbial ecosystems and take steps to protect them. This chapter discusses the importance of biodiversity, highlighting the need to conserve microbial ecosystems as a foundation for planetary health. It also explores the role of businesses in promoting microbial conservation, for example, through sustainable sourcing and responsible land use.

The invisible guardians of the environment, microorganisms play a vital role in maintaining the health of our planet. By supporting their natural processes, businesses can contribute to a more sustainable future. This chapter concludes by emphasizing the importance of recognizing and protecting the role of microorganisms as environmental guardians.

10

Chapter 10: The Microbial Revolution

The 21st century is witnessing a microbial revolution, where these tiny organisms are being harnessed to address some of the world's most pressing challenges. From climate change to resource scarcity, microorganisms offer innovative solutions that are both effective and sustainable. This chapter explores the cutting-edge technologies that are driving this revolution, from synthetic biology to microbiome engineering.

One of the most exciting developments in the microbial revolution is synthetic biology. This field involves designing and engineering microorganisms to perform specific functions, such as producing biofuels or cleaning up pollution. This chapter examines the potential of synthetic biology to transform industries, create new markets, and redefine the relationship between business and the environment.

Another area of innovation is microbiome engineering. The microbiome, the community of microorganisms that live in and on our bodies, plays a crucial role in human health. By engineering the microbiome, scientists can develop new treatments for diseases and improve overall health. This chapter explores how businesses are leveraging microbiome engineering to create innovative healthcare solutions, from probiotics to personalized medicine.

The microbial revolution is also driving advancements in agriculture. By engineering soil microbiomes, scientists can enhance soil health, improve crop yields, and reduce the need for chemical inputs. This chapter discusses the potential of microbiome engineering to create sustainable agricultural practices, benefiting both the economy and the environment.

However, the microbial revolution is not without its risks. The manipulation of microorganisms raises ethical and safety concerns, particularly when it comes to genetically modified organisms. This chapter explores the potential risks associated with microbial technologies and discusses strategies for mitigating them. Collaboration between businesses, governments, and research institutions is essential to ensure that the microbial revolution is conducted responsibly.

The microbial revolution represents a paradigm shift in how we think about sustainability. By harnessing the power of microorganisms, businesses can create innovative solutions that address both economic and environmental challenges. This chapter concludes by emphasizing the importance of investing in microbial technologies and fostering a culture of innovation. As we move forward, the microbial revolution will play an increasingly important role in shaping a sustainable future.

11

Chapter 11: The Business of Biodiversity

Biodiversity is often associated with visible life forms, such as plants and animals, but microorganisms are the true champions of diversity. They represent the vast majority of genetic and functional diversity on Earth, making them a treasure trove of potential for businesses. This chapter explores the business case for biodiversity, focusing on the untapped potential of microbial diversity.

One of the key benefits of microbial biodiversity is its potential for bioprospecting. Bioprospecting involves searching for valuable biological resources, such as new drugs, enzymes, and biofuels. This chapter examines how businesses are using bioprospecting to unlock the potential of microbial diversity, creating innovative products and services that benefit both the economy and the environment.

Another area where microbial biodiversity is making a difference is in agriculture. By harnessing the diversity of soil microbes, businesses can develop sustainable agricultural practices that enhance soil health and improve crop yields. This chapter explores how businesses are leveraging microbial biodiversity to create innovative solutions for the agriculture industry, from biofertilizers to pest control.

Microbial biodiversity also plays a key role in maintaining ecosystem health. From the soil to the oceans, microbes are essential for processes like nutrient cycling, carbon sequestration, and water purification. This chapter discusses how businesses can support microbial biodiversity, for example, by adopting sustainable land use practices and protecting natural habitats.

However, the business of biodiversity is not without its challenges. Bioprospecting raises ethical and legal questions, particularly when it comes to the ownership and use of genetic resources. This chapter explores the ethical and legal considerations associated with bioprospecting and discusses strategies for addressing them. Collaboration between businesses, governments, and indigenous communities is essential to ensure that bioprospecting is conducted responsibly.

The business of biodiversity offers immense potential for innovation and sustainability. By harnessing the power of microbial diversity, businesses can create innovative solutions that address both economic and environmental challenges. This chapter concludes by emphasizing the importance of investing in microbial biodiversity and fostering a culture of conservation. As we move forward, the business of biodiversity will play an increasingly important role in shaping a sustainable future.

12

Chapter 12: A New Partnership

As we look to the future, it is clear that microorganisms will play an increasingly important role in shaping sustainable business practices. This final chapter reflects on the journey of discovery and innovation that has brought us to this point. It calls for a new partnership between businesses and microorganisms, one that is based on mutual respect and shared goals.

The partnership between businesses and microorganisms is not just about harnessing their capabilities; it is about recognizing their value as silent stakeholders. Microorganisms have been shaping the world for billions of years, and their role in sustainability is only now being fully appreciated. This chapter emphasizes the importance of viewing microorganisms as partners, rather than tools, in the quest for sustainability.

The new partnership between businesses and microorganisms requires a shift in mindset. Businesses must move beyond traditional approaches to sustainability and embrace innovative solutions that are rooted in the principles of nature. This chapter explores how businesses can adopt a holistic approach to sustainability, balancing economic, environmental, and social considerations.

Collaboration is key to the success of this new partnership. Businesses must work together with researchers, policymakers, and communities to unlock the full potential of microbial technologies. This chapter discusses the importance of interdisciplinary collaboration, highlighting the need for biologists, engineers, and business leaders to work together to create sustainable solutions.

The new partnership between businesses and microorganisms also requires a commitment to ethical practices. Businesses must ensure that their use of microbial technologies is conducted responsibly, with respect for the natural world and the communities that depend on it. This chapter explores the ethical considerations associated with microbial technologies and discusses strategies for addressing them.

The new partnership between businesses and microorganisms offers immense potential for innovation and sustainability. By working together, we can create a future where businesses thrive by working in harmony with the natural world, guided by the silent stakeholders that have always been there, quietly shaping our world. This chapter concludes with a vision of a sustainable future, where businesses and microorganisms work together to create a better world for all.

Book Description: Silent Stakeholders: The Role of Microorganisms in Sustainable Business Practices

In a world where sustainability is no longer a choice but a necessity, *Silent Stakeholders* uncovers the untapped potential of the smallest yet most powerful life forms on Earth: microorganisms. These invisible architects of life have been shaping ecosystems for billions of years, and now, they hold the key to revolutionizing how businesses operate in harmony with the planet.

This thought-provoking book takes readers on a journey into the microbial world, exploring how bacteria, fungi, algae, and other microorganisms are driving innovation across industries. From transforming waste into valuable resources to producing sustainable fuels, plastics, and food, microbes are proving to be indispensable allies in the quest for a greener future. Each chapter delves into real-world applications, showcasing how businesses are harnessing microbial technologies to reduce environmental impact, cut costs, and create circular economies.

But *Silent Stakeholders* goes beyond the science. It challenges readers to rethink the ethical implications of microbial exploitation, urging businesses to

CHAPTER 12: A NEW PARTNERSHIP

adopt practices that respect these tiny life forms as partners rather than tools. With a blend of scientific insight, business strategy, and ethical reflection, this book offers a roadmap for building a sustainable future—one where businesses thrive by working in harmony with nature's silent stakeholders.

Whether you're a business leader, an environmental advocate, or simply curious about the hidden forces shaping our world, *Silent Stakeholders* will inspire you to see microorganisms in a new light—and to recognize their profound role in creating a sustainable tomorrow.

www.ingramcontent.com/pod-product-compliance
Lightning Source LLC
LaVergne TN
LVHW020744090526
838202LV00057BA/6226